SILLY JOKES FOR FUNNY KIDS

BUSTER

Illustrated by
Andrew Pinder

Compiled by Josephine Southon

Edited by Zoe Clark

Designed by Derrian Bradder

Cover design by Jake Da'Costa

First published in Great Britain in 2022 by Buster Books,
an imprint of Michael O'Mara Books Limited,
9 Lion Yard, Tremadoc Road, London SW4 7NQ

W www.mombooks.com/buster   f Buster Books   🐦 @BusterBooks   📷 @buster_books

A CIP catalogue record for this book is available from the British Library.

ISBN: 978-1-78055-908-7

2 4 6 8 10 9 7 5 3

This product is made of material from well-managed, FSC®-certified
forests and other controlled sources. The manufacturing processes
conform to the environmental regulations of the country of origin.

This book was printed in June 2023 by
CPI Group (UK) Ltd, Croydon, CR0 4YY.

FSC
www.fsc.org
MIX
Paper | Supporting
responsible forestry
FSC® C171272

CONTENTS

Introduction

Why couldn't the hamburger stop cracking jokes?

He was on a roll.

Welcome to this te he he-larious collection of the silliest jokes for funny kids.

In this book you will find over 300 rib-tickling roarers which will have you laughing your socks off – from zany zingers and belly laughin' LOLs to alien antics and hilarious head scratchers.

If these jokes don't tickle your funny bone then nothing will. Don't forget to share your favourites with your friends and family and have them howling with laughter, too!

GROSS GIGGLES

What do you call a farting fairy?

Stinkerbell.

**What smells gross and
makes a sound like a bell?**

Dung.

**What do you call a cat
who eats beans?**

Puss in Toots.

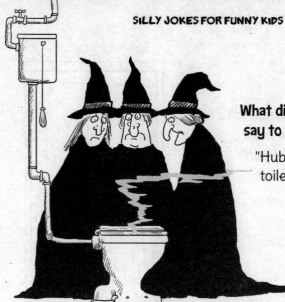

What did the witches say to the plumber?

"Hubble bubble, toilet trouble!"

What do you call a bogey in space?

An astrosnot.

What do you do if you find a bear in your toilet?

Let it finish!

What do you call a teacher who doesn't fart in public?

A private tooter.

Why did the baker smell bad?

Because he kneaded a poo.

How do you stop your nose from running?

Take away its shoes.

What did the poo say to the fart?

"You blow me away."

What comes out of your nose at 150 kmph?

A Lambogreeny.

**Why was the
sand wet?**

Because the
sea weed.

**Why did the bogey
cross the road?**

Because it was
getting picked on.

**Why did the fart get
expelled from school?**

Its attitude stank.

Did you hear about the outfit made of slime?

It was hard to pull off.

Why do ducks have tail feathers?

To cover their buttquacks.

Did you hear about the TV show *Constipated*?

It never came out.

**What did the baby
slime say to its dad?**

"Goo goo."

**What did one fly say to
the other fly at lunch?**

"Is this stool taken?"

Why was the nose sad?

Because it didn't
get picked.

Why shouldn't you fart on the stairs?

It's wrong on so many levels.

What did the bogey say to its girlfriend?

"I'm stuck on you."

Who are the most dangerous farters?

Ninjas – they're silent but deadly.

What did the policeman say to the toilet thief?

"Urine trouble!"

How do you recognize two slimes in love?

They're practically glued together.

What do you do when you run out of bubble bath?

Eat beans for dinner.

What's another name for a snail?

A slug wearing a helmet.

Knock, Knock.

Who's there?

I eat mop.

I eat mop, who?

You eat your poo? Gross!

There are two reasons you should never drink toilet water ...

... Number one and number two.

Why did the slime stay at home?

He had no place to goo.

Why was the toilet seat upset?

It had just been dumped.

What do you call a skinny bogey?

Slim pickings.

**What do you get
when a queen farts?**

A noble gas.

Did you pick your nose?

No, I was born with it!

**Why were there
balloons in the toilet?**

Because there was
a birthday potty.

17

What's a bee's favourite sports lesson?

Rug-bee.

Why couldn't the music teacher open the classroom door?

His keys were on the piano.

What do you do if a teacher rolls their eyes at you?

Pick them up and roll them back.

What did the ghost teacher say to the class?

"Look at the board and I'll go through it again."

Why did the students study on the airplane?

They wanted higher marks.

Why doesn't the Sun need to go to college?

Because it has one million degrees.

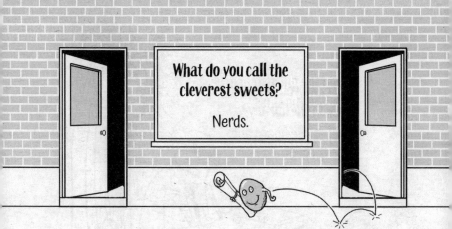

What do you call the cleverest sweets?

Nerds.

Why did the boy eat his homework?

Because the teacher said it was a piece of cake.

Why are singing coaches good at baseball?

They have perfect pitch.

21

Why can't you keep a
clock in the library?

It tocks too much.

What's the worst thing
that can happen to a
geography teacher?

Getting lost.

Why did the dog do
so well in school?

Because he was the
teacher's pet.

Teacher: You've got your shoes on the wrong feet.

Student: But these are the only feet I've got.

Why did the egg get sent out of class?

He kept telling yolks.

What flies around the classroom at night?

The alpha-BAT.

23

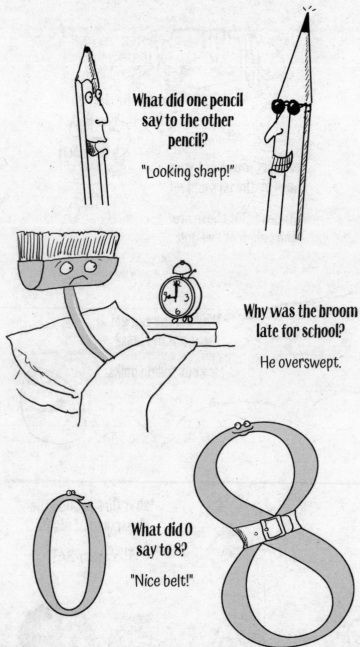

What did one pencil say to the other pencil?

"Looking sharp!"

Why was the broom late for school?

He overswept.

What did 0 say to 8?

"Nice belt!"

Why did the clock in the cafeteria run slow?

It always went back four seconds.

Where does a librarian sleep?

Between the covers.

Why didn't the skeleton go to the school dance?

He had no body to go with.

What do you call a
student with a pocket
encyclopedia?

Smartie pants.

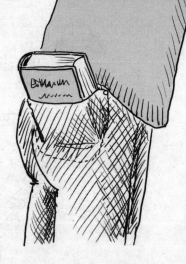

What does a thesaurus
eat for breakfast?

A synonym bun.

Why did the teacher
jump into the pool?

To test the waters.

**Why did the square
go to the gym?**

To stay in shape.

**Why did the boy bring
a ladder to class?**

He wanted to go
to high school.

**Why did the girl cross
the playground?**

To get to the
other slide.

Are monsters good at sums?

Not unless you Count Dracula.

Where did the cat take his students?

To the meow-seum.

Why didn't the skeleton go to school?

His heart wasn't in it.

What did the science book say to the maths book?

"You've got problems."

What position did the ghost play in the school soccer team?

Ghoulie.

Why did the girl eat her homework?

Because she didn't have a dog.

Where do you learn how to make ice cream?

At Sundae school.

Why don't fish do well at school?

Because they work below C-level.

What are the 10 letters of the pirate alphabet?

I, I, R, and the seven Cs.

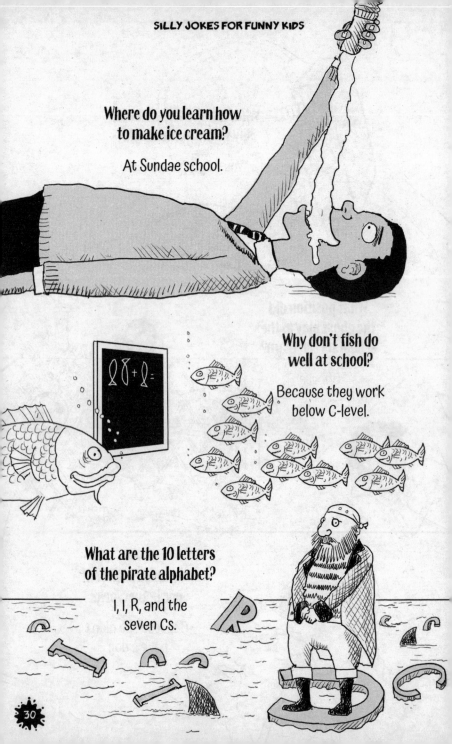

FOOLISH FEASTIN'

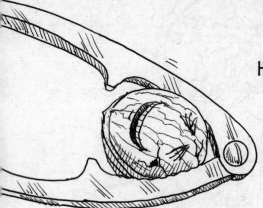

**How do you make
a walnut laugh?**

Crack it up!

**Why did the pepper
stay inside all day?**

He was a
little chilli.

**How do you make
an apple turnover?**

Push it down a hill.

Why did the skeleton go to the BBQ?

To get another rib.

What do you say to a cheese thief?

"That's nacho cheese!"

Which friends should you take to dinner?

Your taste buds.

What do you call
blueberries playing
music together?

A jam session.

What did the tough
guy pepperoni say?

"You wanna pizza me?!"

Did you hear about
the carrot detective?

He got to the root
of every case.

What do you get when you put three ducks in a box?

A box of quackers.

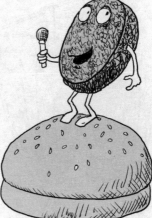

Why couldn't the hamburger stop cracking jokes?

He was on a roll.

What's green and sings rock and roll?

Elvis Parsley.

Did you hear the joke about jam?

Never mind, you might spread it.

What's a vampire's favourite fruit?

Blood oranges.

What's a cheese's favourite music?

R'n'Brie.

Why did the baker go to jail?

He was caught beating the eggs.

How do you know carrots are good for your eyes?

Well, have you ever seen a rabbit wearing glasses?

Why did the shark eat the tight rope walker?

He wanted a balanced meal.

Why did two 4s skip dinner?

Because they already 8.

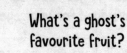

What's a ghost's favourite fruit?

Boo!-berries.

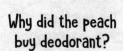

Why did the peach buy deodorant?

To freshen up its pits.

Why was the cake
in a rush?

It was running
choco-late.

How do you make
a milkshake?

Give it a
good scare.

When was the spaghetti
a piece of dough?

In a pasta life.

How does a cucumber become a pickle?

It goes through a jarring experience.

Why did the wedding cake need a tissue?

It was in tiers.

How do penguins make pancakes?

With their flippers.

40

Why did the orange lose the race?

It ran out of juice.

What did the cupcake say to its icing?

"I'd be muffin without you."

What did the lonely celery
say to the cabbage?

"Please lettuce be friends."

What did the mustard say to the refrigerator?

"Close the door, I'm dressing!"

What's a vampire's favourite soup?

Scream of mushroom.

Why did the melon jump into the lake?

It wanted to be a watermelon.

42

What did the strawberry
say to its crush?

"I'm berry fond of you."

What do you call
a sleeping pizza?

PiZZZZZa.

What do you call
a pan in space?

An unidentified
frying object.

CLOWNIN' AROUND

Why does a flamingo stand on one leg?

Because if it lifted two it would fall over.

How are sports arenas kept cool?

They're filled with fans.

Did you hear about the mathematician who's afraid of negative numbers?

He'll stop at nothing to avoid them.

What did the lightbulb say to its sweetheart?

"I love you a watt."

What did one wall say to the other wall?

"I'll meet you at the corner."

Why did the scarecrow win a prize?

For being outstanding in his field.

What do sprinters eat before a race?

Nothing. They fast.

Why do bicycles fall over?

Because they're two-tired.

How do chickens feel at the end of a long day?

Eggs-hausted.

47

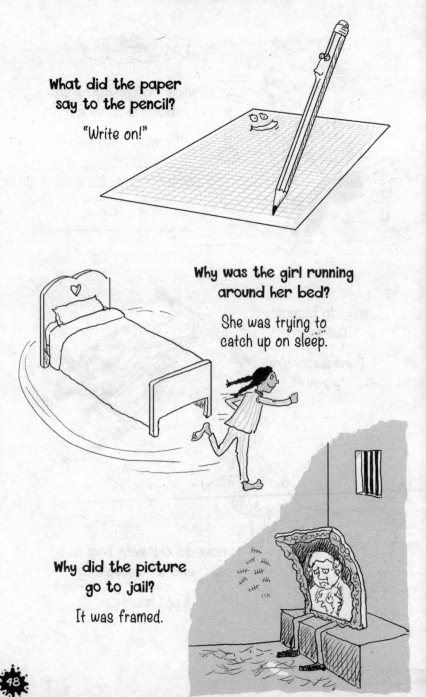

What did the paper
say to the pencil?

"Write on!"

Why was the girl running
around her bed?

She was trying to
catch up on sleep.

Why did the picture
go to jail?

It was framed.

What did one hat say to the other hat?

"Stay here, I'm going on ahead."

Why do shoelaces never win races?

Because they're always tied.

What kind of shoes do ninjas wear?

Sneakers.

How do billboards communicate?

With sign language.

Why do witches wear black?

So you can't tell which witch is which.

What did the traffic light say to the car?

"Don't look, I'm changing!"

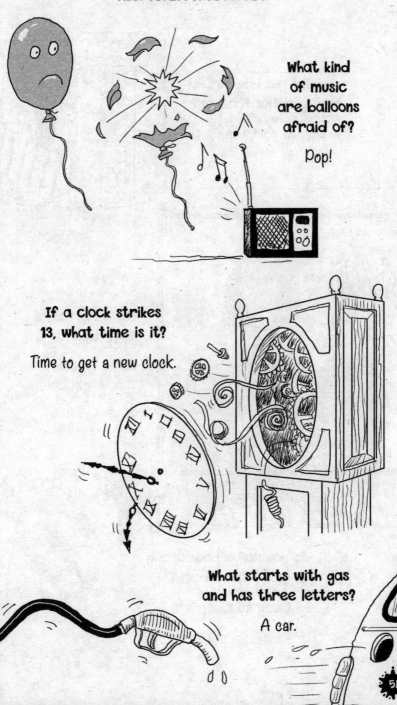

What kind
of music
are balloons
afraid of?

Pop!

If a clock strikes
13, what time is it?

Time to get a new clock.

What starts with gas
and has three letters?

A car.

51

Why did the boy put his money in the freezer?

He wanted cold, hard cash.

I'm a big fan of whiteboards ...

... They're re-markable!

What do you call a boomerang that won't come back?

A stick.

Why can't you trust an atom?

They make up everything.

Why are basketball courts always wet?

Because of all the dribbling.

Why did the doctor get mad?

She'd run out of patients.

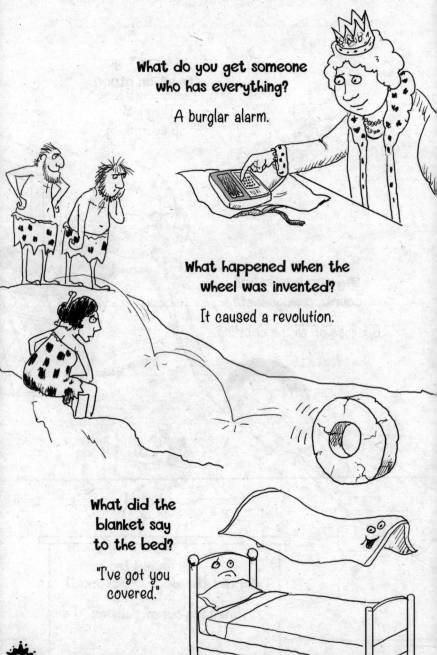

What do you get someone
who has everything?

A burglar alarm.

What happened when the
wheel was invented?

It caused a revolution.

What did the
blanket say
to the bed?

"I've got you
covered."

Why are robots fearless?

They have nerves of steel.

Why did the computer go to the dentist?

It had a bluetooth.

What do you call an old snowman?

Water.

Why do Christmas elves go to music class?

To improve their wrapping skills.

Why did Mozart sell his chickens?

Because they kept saying, "Bach, Bach, Bach."

I went to buy some camouflage shorts the other day ...

... I couldn't find any.

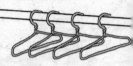

WILD 'N' WACKY

What did the tree say to the woodpecker?

"Leaf me alone!"

What do you get when you cross a snail with a porcupine?

A slowpoke.

Why do bees have sticky hair?

From the honeycombs.

What do you call a huge pile of cats?

A meow-ntain.

What did the duck say after buying lipstick?

"Put it on my bill."

Why couldn't the pony sing?

Because she was a little hoarse.

How do you keep a bull from charging?

Take away its credit card.

How did the lobster reach the ocean?

By shell-icopter.

How do mountains stay warm in winter?

They wear icecaps.

What do you call a funny chicken?

A comedi-hen.

What's a tree's least favourite month?

Sep-TIMBERRR.

What do you call a sheep with no legs?

A cloud.

What do you call a kitten's reflection?

A copycat.

Why did the bird get in trouble at school?

For tweeting on a test.

What did one firefly say to the other firefly?

"You glow, girl!"

What do you call a tornado full of cats?

A cat-astrophe.

When do monkeys fall from the sky?

During Ape-ril showers.

What do you call two spiders who just got married?

Newly-webs.

What do you call an ant who fights crime?

A vigil-ant-e.

Why did the teacher buy birdseed?

For her parrot-teacher conference.

How does a hurricane see?

With its eye.

What do you call a flower that runs on electricity?

A power plant.

Which animal is out of bounds?

An exhausted kangaroo.

What did the limestone say to the geologist?

"Don't take me for granite!"

What did the big walnut tree say to the little walnut tree?

"I will nut stand for this behaviour!"

What's the laziest mountain in the world?

Mount Ever-rest.

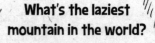

Where does the Sun go at night?

Keep looking, it'll dawn on you soon.

**How does the rain
tie its shoes?**

With rainbows.

**Why couldn't the gardener
plant any flowers?**

Because she
hadn't botany.

**What's the difference between
a horse and the weather?**

One is reined up, the
other rains down.

Why should you never hire lightning for a job?

It's always on strike.

What happens to maple trees on Valentine's Day?

They get sappy.

Why did the girl leave her house with only one boot on?

She heard there would be a 50% chance of snow.

When does it rain money?

When there's change in the weather.

How do you say goodbye to a curly haired dog?

"Poodle-oo!"

Why shouldn't you start a fight with a cloud?

It'll storm out on you.

ALIEN ANTICS

How do you get an astronaut's
baby to stop crying?

You rocket.

How do you throw the
best party on Mars?

Planet.

What do you give an
angry astronaut?

Lots of space.

Where did the astronaut store her sandwich?

In her launch box.

Which planet is the best singer?

Nep-tune.

What did the astronaut say to the three-headed alien?

"Hello. Hello. Hello."

Why did the peanut go to space school?

He wanted to become an astro-nut.

What did the astronaut say to their rocket ship?

"You're a blast!"

What did Venus say to Saturn?

"Give me a ring sometime."

73

What do astronauts use to eat their meals?

Satellite dishes.

What do you do when you see a spaceman?

Park in it, man.

What did one shooting star say to the other shooting star?

"Pleased to meteor!"

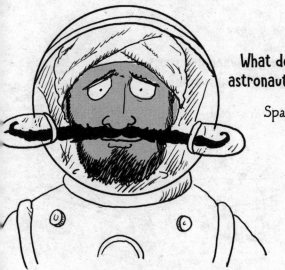

What do you call an astronaut's moustache?

Spacial hair.

What do aliens have for brunch?

Poached eggs-traterrestrials on toast.

How do aliens write poems?

In uni-verses.

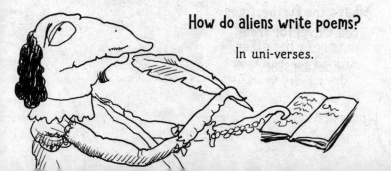

What do you get when you cross an alien with a kangaroo?

A Mars-upial.

Why don't aliens eat clowns?

Because they taste funny.

What's the furthest you can travel for free?

Around the Sun (you do it every year).

Einstein developed a theory about space ...

... About time, too!

Did you hear about the claustrophobic astronaut?

He just needed a little space.

Of all the planets, Saturn has the best name ...

... It has a nice ring to it.

**Why haven't aliens come
to our solar system yet?**

They've read the
one-star reviews.

I'm reading a book about anti-gravity ...

... It's impossible to put down.

**Why are people always
criticizing Orion's belt?**

It's a big waist of space.

How did the alien break his phone?

He Saturn it.

Why is space a good tourist spot?

The view is breathtaking and will leave you speechless.

What do astronauts eat for breakfast?

Spacetries.

Why is the Moon always tired?

Because it stays out all night.

How does the Sun listen to music?

On the ray-dio.

Where do keyboards go for milkshakes?

The space bar.

Why did the star study really hard?

To be brighter.

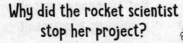

Why did the rocket scientist stop her project?

She had no comet-ment.

What do you call an alien's pet?

An extra-furrestrial.

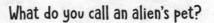

What's green and squishy?

A Martian-mallow.

Not everyone can pull off
wearing a spacesuit ...

... But I rocket.

My sister is obsessed
with the Moon ...

... I'm hoping it's
just a phase.

BELLY LAUGHIN' LOLS

Why are ghosts always hungry?

Food goes right through them.

What do you call a monkey at the North Pole?

Lost.

Did you hear the joke about the roof?

It will go over your head.

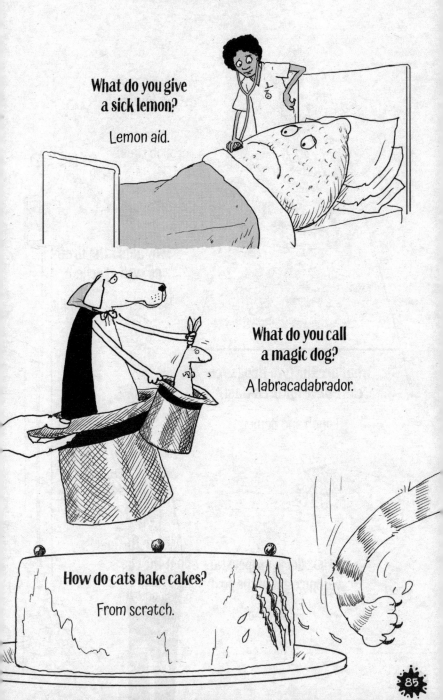

What do you give a sick lemon?

Lemon aid.

What do you call a magic dog?

A labracadabrador.

How do cats bake cakes?

From scratch.

Why didn't the firefly do well at school?

He wasn't very bright.

What are the two things you can't have for breakfast?

Lunch and dinner.

What does a superstar vampire get in the post?

Fangmail.

What's a robot's favourite snack?

Computer chips.

Why was Cinderella not very good at soccer?

Because her coach was a pumpkin.

Why did the woman become an archaeologist?

Because her career was in ruins.

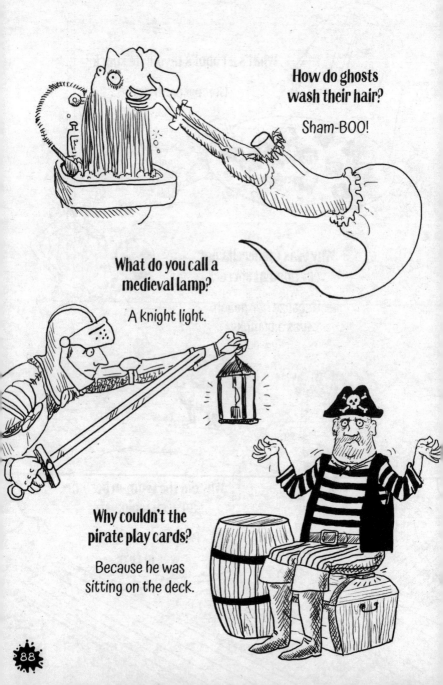

How do ghosts wash their hair?

Sham-BOO!

What do you call a medieval lamp?

A knight light.

Why couldn't the pirate play cards?

Because he was sitting on the deck.

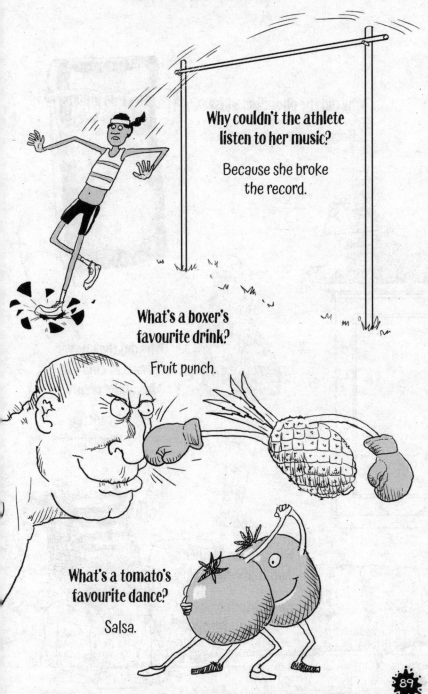

Why couldn't the athlete listen to her music?

Because she broke the record.

What's a boxer's favourite drink?

Fruit punch.

What's a tomato's favourite dance?

Salsa.

Why did the phone get glasses?

Because it lost its contacts.

Why did the lawyer arrive at court in his underwear?

He'd forgotten his lawsuit.

Why did the farmer's son study medicine?

He wanted to go into a different field.

How do poets say hello?

"Hey, haven't we metaphor?"

Why was the monster so full?

He was goblin his pie.

How do musicians keep their teeth clean?

With a tuba toothpaste.

HEAD SCRATCHERS AND TONGUE TWISTERS

**What can fly
without wings?**

Time.

**Where does Friday come
before Thursday?**

The dictionary.

**What can you
catch but
never throw?**

A cold.

What has many rings but no fingers?

A telephone.

What is always in front of you but can't be seen?

The future.

What's something that falls but never hits the ground?

The temperature.

What goes up and down
but doesn't move?

Stairs.

What gets bigger
the more you take
away from it?

A hole.

What can you hold in
your left hand but
not in your right?

Your right elbow.

95

Why is dark spelled with a K and not a C?

Because you can't C in the dark.

What can you break without touching?

A promise.

What is broken when you say its name?

Silence.

What can run but
never walks?

A river.

The more you take, the
more you leave behind.
What are they?

Footsteps.

Which word is spelled
incorrectly in the
dictionary?

Incorrectly.

HOW QUICKLY CAN YOU SAY THESE TONGUE TWISTERS?

Fred fed Ted bread and Ted fed Fred bread.

I saw a saw that could out saw any other saw I ever saw.

How many yaks could a yak pack pack, if a yak pack could pack yaks?

Seventy-seven benevolent elephants.

Imagine an imaginary menagerie manager managing an imaginary menagerie.

A synonym for cinnamon is a cinnamon synonym.

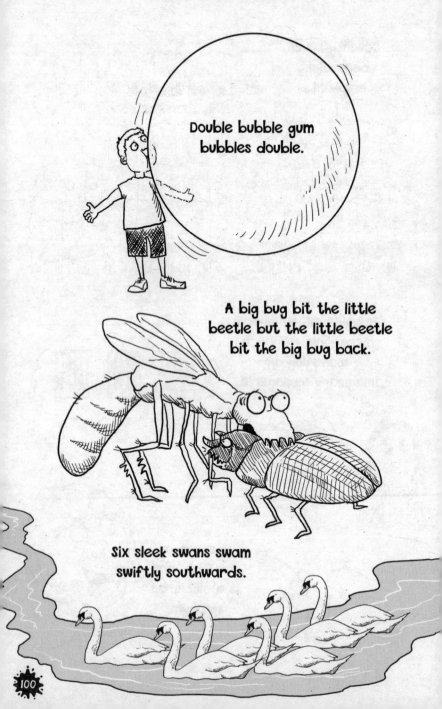

We surely shall see the Sun shine soon.

Any noise annoys an oyster but a noisy noise annoys an oyster more.

Five frantic frogs fled from fifty fierce fishes.

BODY BANTER

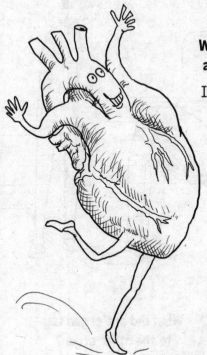

Why is the heart a good dancer?

It always stays on the beat.

What did the left eye say to the right eye?

Between us, something smells.

When does a brain feel afraid?

When it loses its nerve.

I don't think I need a spine ...

... It's holding me back.

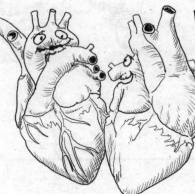

What did one organ say to the other organ?

Let's have a heart to heart.

Why did the one-handed man cross the road?

To get to the second-hand shop.

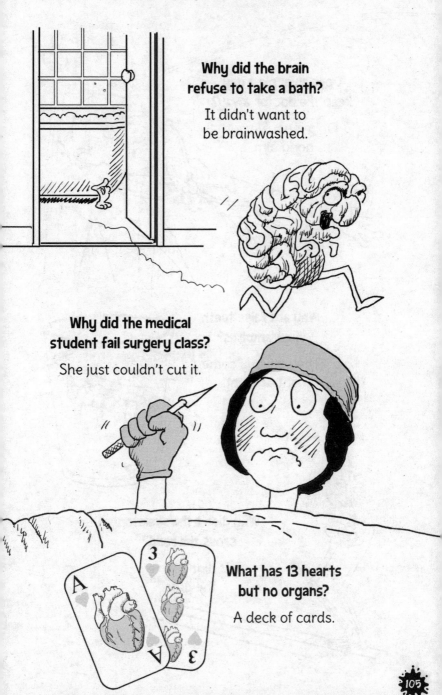

Why did the brain refuse to take a bath?

It didn't want to be brainwashed.

Why did the medical student fail surgery class?

She just couldn't cut it.

What has 13 hearts but no organs?

A deck of cards.

Does an apple a day keep the doctor away?

Only if you've got good aim.

Why are false teeth like vampires?

They always come out at night.

Why didn't the skeleton cross the road?

It didn't have the guts.

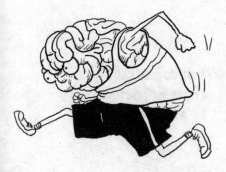

Why did the brain go for a run?

To jog its memory.

Why did the doctor take a red pen to work?

In case she needed to draw blood.

"Is that a rabbit on your head?"

"No, it's just my hare."

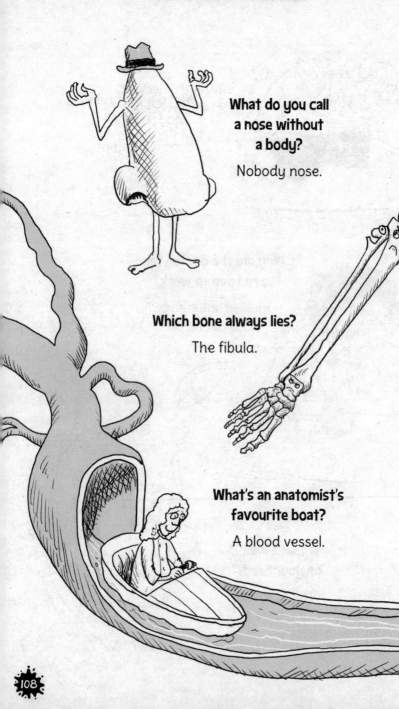

What do you call a nose without a body?

Nobody nose.

Which bone always lies?

The fibula.

What's an anatomist's favourite boat?

A blood vessel.

Why is the nervous system so reckless?

It does everything on impulse.

What did one lung say to the other lung?

"We be-lung together."

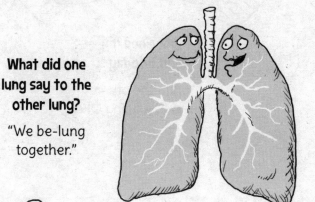

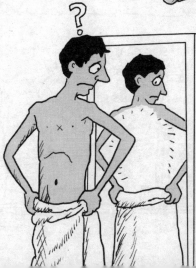

My best friend told me he had my back ...

... I'd been wondering where that went.

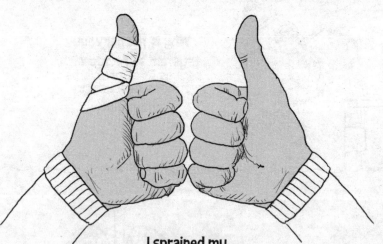

**I sprained my
thumb today ...**

... On the other
hand, I'm doing OK.

**I pulled a muscle
digging for gold ...**

... It's only a
miner injury.

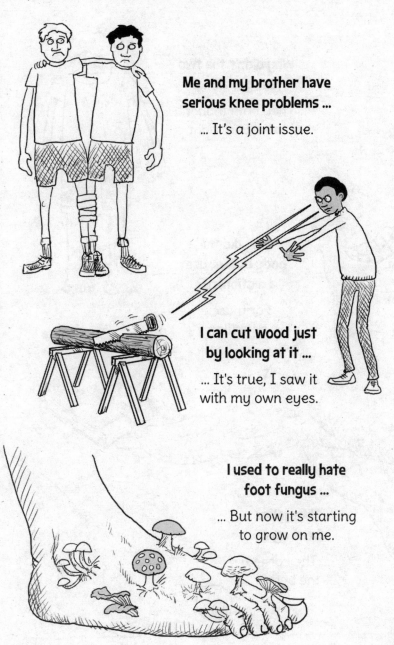

Me and my brother have
serious knee problems ...

... It's a joint issue.

I can cut wood just
by looking at it ...

... It's true, I saw it
with my own eyes.

I used to really hate
foot fungus ...

... But now it's starting
to grow on me.

Why didn't the two feet get along?

They both thought they were right.

Why did the body builder use a dictionary?

For muscle definition.

I like jokes about eyes ...

... The cornea the better.

What do you call a muscly bee?

Beefy.

If a bear wears socks and shoes ...

Does it still have bear feet?

Who brings you toothpaste at Christmas time?

Santa Floss.

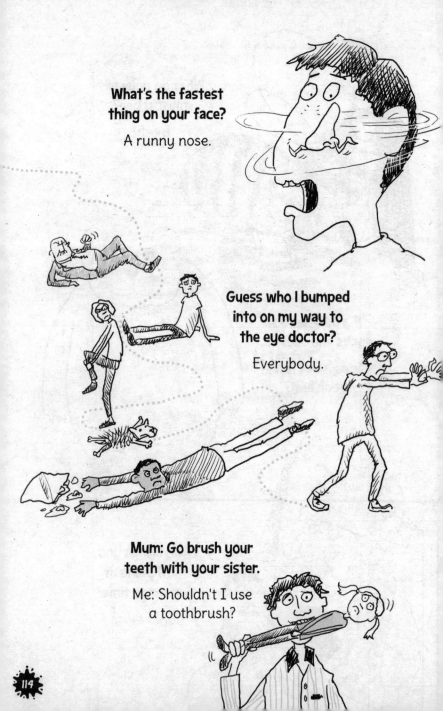

What's the fastest thing on your face?

A runny nose.

Guess who I bumped into on my way to the eye doctor?

Everybody.

Mum: Go brush your teeth with your sister.

Me: Shouldn't I use a toothbrush?

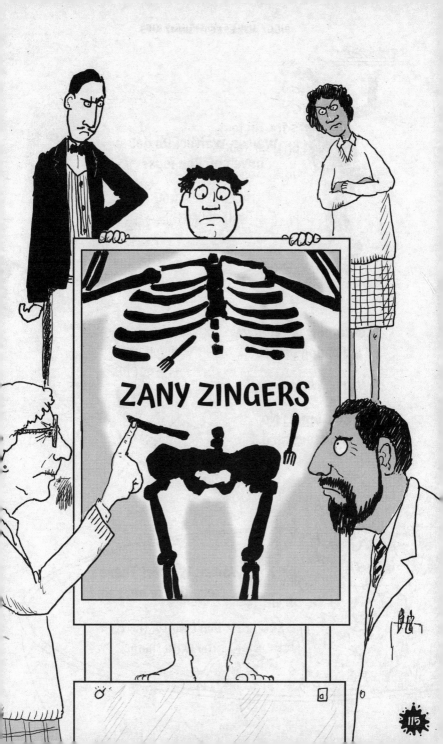

**Waiter, Waiter! Do you
have chicken legs?**

No, sir, I've always
walked like this.

**Customer: Can I have
a hot dog please?**

Waiter: With pleasure.

**Customer: No,
with mustard.**

**Waiter, Waiter! There's
a caterpillar in my salad.**

Don't worry, there's
no extra charge.

Waiter, Waiter! Will my pancakes be long?

No, they will be round.

Customer: Why is there a crocodile in my soup?

Waiter: You told me to make it snappy.

Waiter, Waiter! What's the meaning of this fly in my teacup?

I wouldn't know. I'm a waiter, not a fortune-teller.

Waiter, Waiter! There's a fly in my butter!

Yes sir, it's called a butterfly.

Customer: There's a bee in my alphabet soup.

Waiter: Yes, and you'll find all the other letters in there, too.

Customer: Do you have bacon and eggs on the menu?

Waiter: Of course not, we clean our menus regularly.

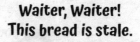

**Waiter, Waiter!
This bread is stale.**

That's odd, it
wasn't last week.

**Waiter: Can I have
your order, please?**

Customer: Of course
not, it's mine!

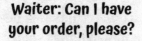

**Waiter, Waiter! Your
tie is in my soup!**

Don't worry, it's
machine washable.

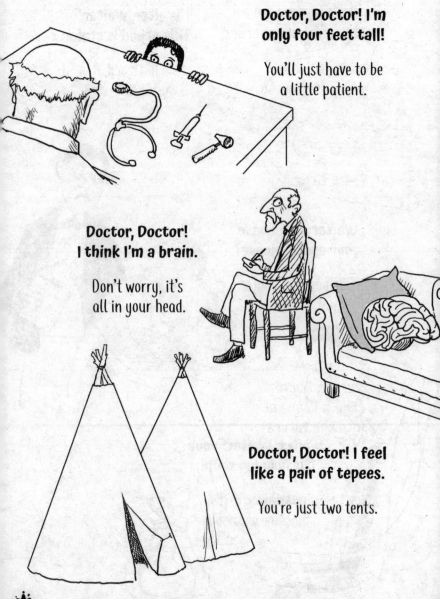

Doctor, Doctor! I'm only four feet tall!

You'll just have to be a little patient.

Doctor, Doctor! I think I'm a brain.

Don't worry, it's all in your head.

Doctor, Doctor! I feel like a pair of tepees.

You're just two tents.

**Doctor, Doctor!
I think I'm a shepherd.**

I wouldn't lose
any sheep over it.

**Doctor, Doctor! Will this
ointment clear up my spots?**

I never make rash promises.

**Doctor, Doctor!
I think I can see
into the future.**

When did this start?

Next Wednesday.

**Doctor, Doctor!
I swallowed a
bone.**

Are you choking?

No, I really did!

**Doctor, Doctor!
I've swallowed my
pocket money.**

Take this and we'll see
if there's any change
in the morning.

**Doctor, Doctor! I've
got a strawberry
stuck in my ear.**

Don't worry, I have
some cream for that.

122

**Doctor, Doctor!
I feel like a dog.**

How long have you
felt like this?

Since I was a puppy.

**Doctor, Doctor! I've
swallowed a watch.**

Take these, they'll help
you pass the time.

**Doctor, Doctor! I feel
like a vampire.**

Take these and you won't
be coffin much longer.

123

Teacher: If I had six oranges in one hand and seven apples in the other, what would I have?

Student: Big hands.

Teacher: Didn't I tell you to stand at the end of the line?

Student: I tried, but there was someone already there.

Teacher: Answer this question at once, what's seven times two?

Student: At once.

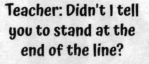

Teacher: You missed school yesterday, didn't you?

Student: To be honest, not really.

Teacher: You know you can't sleep in class.

Student: Maybe if you were a little quieter, I could.

Teacher: I hope I didn't see you looking at Jacob's answers.

Student: I hope so, too.

Teacher: Name two pronouns.

Student: Who? Me?

Teacher: Correct!

Teacher: We will have half a day of school this morning.

Students: Hooray!

Teacher: We will have the other half this afternoon.

Teacher: I've sent you to the headteacher every day this week. What do you have to say for yourself?

Student: I'm glad it's Friday!

Teacher: Where are the Great Plains located?

Student: At the great airports.

Teacher: What is the chemical formula for water?

Student: H-I-J-K-L-M-N-O.

Teacher: What are you talking about?

Student: Yesterday you said it was H to O.

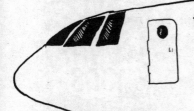

Teacher: Please could you pay a little attention?

Student: I am, I'm paying as little attention as I can.

127

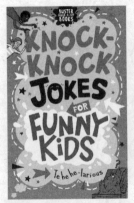

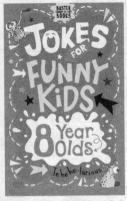